Our Honor Defend®
The Greatest Stories of
Ohio State Football

Our Honor Defend®

The Greatest Stories of Ohio State Football

Emily Stover

Published in 2025 by Sophia Drive LLC

Text copyright © 2025 by Emily Stover

ISBN: 979-8-9988329-0-1
First Edition, 2025

Author: Emily Stover
Illustrations and Design: Geoff Stover

This publication is designed to provide accurate and authoritative information in regard to the subject matter covered. The publisher and author are not associated with, and specifically disclaim any endorsement of any teams, entities, players, or other persons referred to herein.

This book contains licensed material from The Ohio State University. All trademarks and service marks displayed are the property of their respective owners and are used herein with permission.

For my four wonderful children Ava, Kara, Ellie and Caleb. Life is so much fun with you! To my husband Geoff, the biggest Buckeye fan of all. And Sadie, who curled up next to me every time I sat down to write.

Contents

1. **A Cinderella Story** – *Heroes of the 2014 National Championship* **11**

2. **"Holy Buckeye!"** – *Craig Krenzel's Pass to Michael Jenkins Saves a Championship Season* **23**

Time Out for Tradition | Carmen Ohio

3. **Breaking The U** – *The Win That Ended a Hurricane Dynasty* **32**

4. **Because I Couldn't Go for 3** – A *Legend of Woody Hayes* **43**

5. **Coming Up Roses** – *Joe Germaine's 1997 Game-Winning Rose Bowl Drive* **52**

Time Out for Tradition | Brutus Buckeye

6. **A Picture Worth a Thousand Words**
 – *Eddie George vs. Notre Dame*   **61**

Time Out for Tradition | Buckeye Leaf Helmet Stickers

7. **Ohio State Against the World** – *Jack Sawyer's Scoop-and-Score Launches Bucks to a National Championship*   **72**

8. **The G.O.A.T.** – *Archie Griffin Plays as a Freshman*   **85**

Time Out for Tradition | Heisman Trophy Winners

9. **A Lost Shoe in the 'Shoe** – *Keith Byars Seals the Comeback Against Illinois*   **92**

10. **The Call That Stood** – *J.T. Barrett Battles Michigan in Double Overtime*   **101**

Time Out for Tradition | History of the Gold Pants Club

11. **EARLE** – *Beating Michigan for Coach Bruce*   **115**

Time Out for Tradition | Script Ohio

Look for these boxes as you read to dive deeper into each story

 Keys to the Game!

Bold words in each story explained at the end of each chapter

Fact Blitz!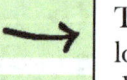

A quick, fun, football fact!

Huddle Up!

Take a closer look at important details in the story

Time Out for Tradition

Learn more about the richest traditions of Ohio State Football

Ohio Stadium, also known as "The Horseshoe," is the home field of The Ohio State Buckeyes football team

A Cinderella Story

Heroes of the 2014 National Championship

I n 2014, Ohio State fans couldn't believe the bad news. Just a few weeks before the football season was about to begin, starting quarterback

Braxton Miller injured his shoulder in practice. He'd miss the whole season. The Buckeyes would have to rely on backup quarterback J.T. Barrett. It turned out that Barrett, a **redshirt** freshman, was cool and ready. In the team's first 11 games, they only lost one. Full of confidence, Barrett and the Buckeyes walked into the Horseshoe ahead of the season's last game ready to beat archrival Michigan.

The game was promising. As the fourth quarter began, the Buckeyes found themselves ahead 28-21. Suddenly, things took a terrible turn. Barrett was brought down hard on a routine running play. He awkwardly crumbled to the ground after being tackled by three Michigan defenders. They got up quickly—but Barrett stayed down. Fans watched in horror as he was given an inflatable cast and carted off the field with a broken ankle. Barrett, too, was now out for the season.

Ohio State fans were devastated. It was lucky their backup quarterback had been so good. What were the chances of a third star quarterback sitting on the bench?

Fact Blitz!

Head coach Urban Meyer had the idea to cover the classic red stripe on the helmets of new Ohio State players with black tape. When players prove their commitment to the team in practice, the black is then removed, as a symbol that they have officially joined the team.

© Photo by Jason Mowry/Icon Sportswire via AP Images

Fans didn't know much about Cardale Jones, the team's third-string quarterback. Head coach Urban Meyer decided to play it safe, finishing the game with a few running plays that didn't require too much from Jones. That day it was enough to beat Michigan. Ohio State won going away 42-28. Now came a bigger test. The Buckeyes were off to a championship game in their conference, the Big Ten. Fans wondered, was Jones up to the challenge?

The Big Ten Championship Game against the Wisconsin Badgers was critical. The Buckeyes were hoping to get selected for a place in the College Football Playoff. However, only the four best college football teams in the country would be chosen for a chance to compete for the national championship. After beating Michigan, Ohio State was ranked sixth in the country. That put them two spots away from the playoff field. It would be hard to leapfrog other strong teams, especially when they were down to their third-string quarterback. The Buckeyes needed a BIG win over Wisconsin to have any hope.

Knowing they would have to be aggressive, Jones and company came out firing. On just the sixth play of the game, Jones struck with a 39-yard touchdown pass. Then, late in the first quarter, running back Ezekiel Elliott burst through the Badger defense for an 81-yard touchdown run. Ohio State scored three more touchdowns and a field goal in the second quarter. At halftime, the Buckeyes had a big 38-0 lead. Fans were euphoric, football experts were befuddled, and the Buckeyes weren't finished.

Jones seemed unstoppable. In the second half, he led three more touchdown drives. The final score was a 59-0 **shutout** over the Badgers. It was one of the biggest blowouts in Big Ten history, and it got the Buckeyes what they wanted: a spot as one of the four best teams in the country.

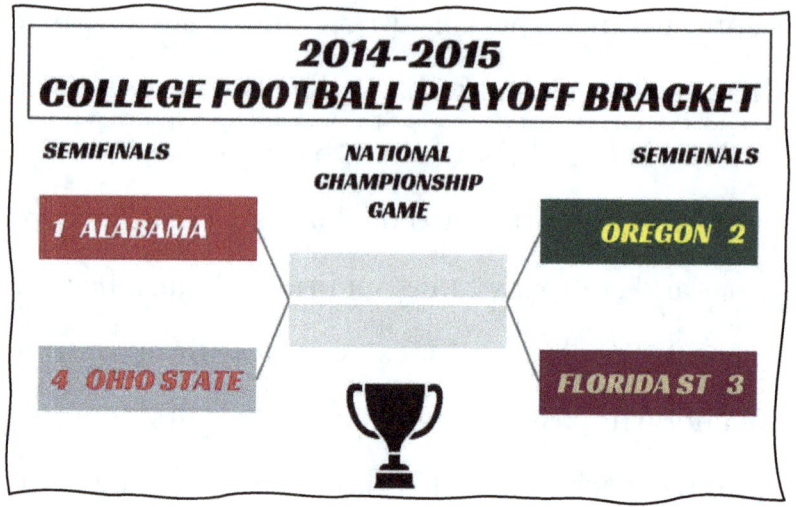

The win against Wisconsin was amazing, but the Buckeyes had no time to enjoy it. They had drawn No. 1 Alabama in the first round. The Alabama Crimson Tide had won three of the last five national championships and had only seven losses in seven years! They were the kings of college football. Even the *location* of the game was intimidating. It was set to be played in the Superdome—a large stadium in Louisiana, just a few hours from Alabama. The Buckeyes were double-digit

underdogs, and they would have to tangle with the Tide on southern turf. The Wisconsin win was a nice story, but most expected the Buckeyes' season to end with a thud against mighty Alabama.

By the second quarter of the game that appeared to be true. The Tide led 21-6 and Alabama fans felt pretty good. However, Ohio State still had their Wisconsin magic. The Buckeyes stormed back, scoring the next four touchdowns! First, Elliott scored on a short run. Then, wide receiver Evan Spencer threw a touchdown to wide receiver Michael Thomas on a trick play. Next, Cardale Jones threw a long touchdown to wide receiver Devin Smith. Then to top it off, defensive end Steve Miller sent fans into a frenzy with a **pick six** late in the third quarter. Alabama was spinning from the barrage of Buckeyes scores. Ohio State was now on top 34-21.

The excitement was building, but Ohio State

wasn't out of the woods yet. An Alabama touchdown late in the third quarter made the score 34-28. Then, an Alabama punt pinned Ohio State back on their own 5-yard line late in the fourth quarter. If the Buckeye offense stalled, the Tide would get the ball and a chance to pull ahead.

Over the next three plays, the Buckeyes moved 10 yards, barely getting a first down so they could keep the ball. Unfortunately, they were still at their own 15-yard line—85 yards from the end zone. Jones took the snap and handed the ball off to Elliott. Spencer came running across the field and laid a key block on two Alabama defenders, opening up a hole. Elliott saw it immediately. He burst through the opening and raced down the sideline.

As he ran, his eyes locked on the giant live jumbotron only to see a trail of helpless Alabama defenders chasing his wake. Ohio State fans roared as he finished his 85-yard touchdown run.

It was a crushing blow to the Tide—from one they could not recover. With a final score of 42-35, the Buckeyes were off to take on Oregon for the national championship!

© Crystal LoGiudice - Imagn Images

Ohio State Buckeyes running back Ezekiel Elliott pulls away from Alabama Crimson Tide defensive back Nick Perry and defensive back Cyrus Jones for an 85-yard touchdown in the fourth quarter of the 2015 Sugar Bowl

Two weeks later, the Buckeyes got their fairy tale ending. They beat Oregon 42-20 in the championship game. Wisconsin → Alabama → Oregon. That unforgettable victory run easily makes

J.T. Barrett, Cardale Jones, Ezekiel Elliott, and the rest of the players on this storied squad one of the most well-known and loved teams in the history of Ohio State.

♟ *Huddle Up!*

Elliott's 85-yard touchdown run against Alabama was later described by popular Ohio State football blog Eleven Warriors as, "85 yards through the heart of the South." Not only did the play unfold down the sideline of the Louisiana Superdome, but it also gave the Buckeyes a jolt of energy, helping them slay the No. 1 Alabama Crimson Tide, a giant that was once thought unbeatable.

Ohio State Buckeyes quarterback Cardale Jones holds the College Football Playoff trophy after beating the Oregon Ducks in the 2015 National Championship Game

 # *Keys to the Game!*

redshirt - a strategic move by a player to delay their participation for one full season, giving them more time to develop their physical and mental skills. This better prepares them for a possible professional career, while still allowing them to compete for four years in the sport.

shutout – a game where the losing team fails to score.

underdog – a team that is thought to have less chance of winning.

pick six – when the defense intercepts the ball (a "pick") and runs it back for a touchdown (six quick points!)

"Holy Buckeye!"

*Craig Krenzel's Pass to Michael Jenkins Saves
a Championship Season*

I f there was ever a word to sum up Ohio State
football games in the year 2002, it would be the
word *close*. The Buckeyes were undefeated after 10

games, even though most of them had been nail-biters. Five of the games were won by 7 points or fewer, and two of them ended in a last-second swing to victory. For instance, in the fourth game of the season, the Buckeyes intercepted the ball in the end zone with less than a minute left to beat the Cincinnati Bearcats 23-19. Likewise, in the ninth game of the season, a pick six by the Buckeye defense was Ohio State's only touchdown in a 13-7 narrow victory over Penn State.

Now in their eleventh game, the Ohio State Buckeyes were playing at the home of the Purdue Boilermakers. The wind was a big problem. Long passes zipped easily off course so both teams were forced into running plays and short passing. Fans hunkered down nervously in their seats.

Scoring in these conditions was almost impossible, and it showed. Late in the fourth quarter, Purdue was ahead 6-3. With under 3 minutes to play, Ohio State had the ball midfield. It was third-and-14. The wind swirled with worry. Buckeye quarterback Craig Krenzel knew time was running out. He fired a solid 13-yard pass to tight end Ben Hartsock, who was then tackled just ONE yard shy of the first down. Things looked bleak. Now, at fourth-and-1, they were down to their last chance.

Jim Tressel, the head coach of the Buckeyes at the time, had a decision to make. He needed to gain just one yard. Should he

🏈 Huddle Up!

If there was one thing head coach Jim Tressel was known for (besides his iconic sweater vest) it was his safe play calling. It was often referred to as "Tresselball." He won games by scoring just enough, employing a strong defense, and playing for good field position. He referred to the punt as the most important play in football. He was not flashy, always erring on the side of protecting the ball.

chance a windy 53-yard field goal to tie the game? Should he call another running play? Everyone expected a safe play call from Tressel. Not only was that his coaching style, but the wind was too unpredictable, and the stakes were too high. Another run seemed the most likely choice, and no one would have blamed him for that decision.

With time melting away, Tressel looked to his quarterback and signaled *King Right 64 Y Shallow Swap*... the play would be a pass instead! The whole season was on the line as the ball was snapped. Almost in slow motion, Krenzel dropped back, scanning . . . searching. As the defense closed in around him, he stepped up into the **pocket** and confidently launched the ball 37 yards down the left sideline.

The wind howled but the ball seemed to know exactly where to go. It sailed high in the air and dropped perfectly into the hands of wide receiver

Michael Jenkins in the end zone to score the winning touchdown! Fans erupted in noisy cheers, and Brent Musburger, the ABC television announcer, exclaimed, "Holy Buckeye!"

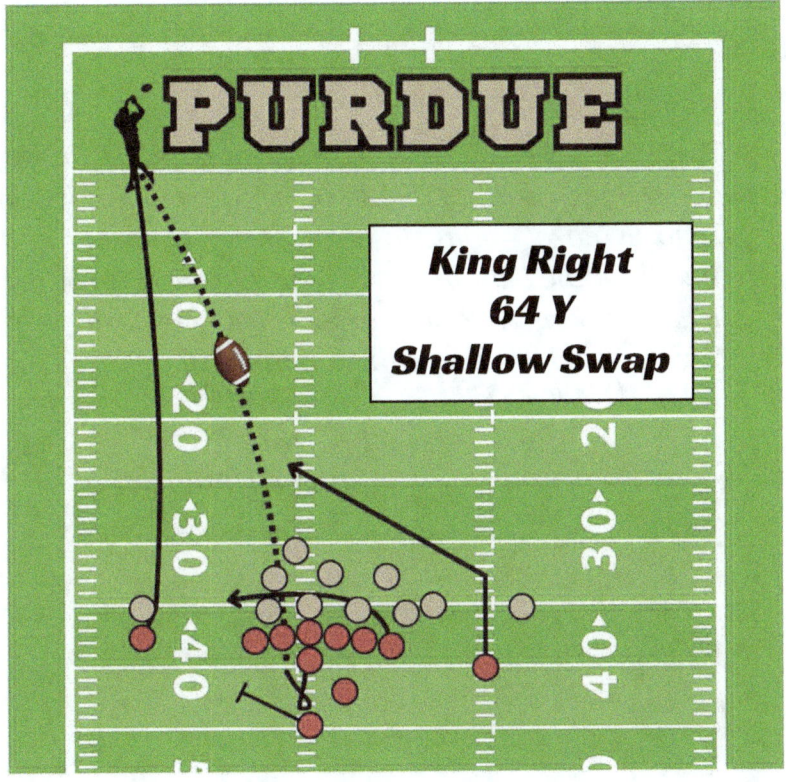

Musburger's memorable phrase that day, coined after the pass to win the Buckeyes the game and save a perfect 11-0 record, will be forever remembered by Ohio State fans all over the world. They can read his legendary play-by-play and recall exactly where they were and how they felt when Craig Krenzel completed that pass to Michael Jenkins.

> *"They're going to show the I-Back behind the fullback here on fourth down. It could be up to the offensive line . . . no, Krenzel's going to throw for it! Gotta get it off! They go for the ballgame . . . Touchdown! Touchdown! Michael Jenkins on fourth-and-1! Would you believe it?! Craig Krenzel strikes with a minute and a half left! HOLY BUCKEYE!"*
>
> *-Brent Musburger*

© *Neal C. Lauron - USA TODAY NETWORK via Imagn Images*

Michael Jenkins catching the pass thrown by quarterback Craig Krenzel for the game winning touchdown against the Boilermakers in 2002

Keys to the Game!

pocket – the area of field created on a passing play where the offensive line forms a wall of protection around the quarterback.

Time Out for Tradition

Carmen Ohio

"Carmen Ohio," Ohio State's alma mater, is one of their oldest school songs. Coach Jim Tressel started a tradition of the football team singing the first verse on the field after every home game. Fans in the stadium link arms, sway, and join in. The song begins with a tune (played by the marching band) that mimics the bells of the Orton Hall tower on campus.

Oh, come let's sing Ohio's praise
and songs to alma mater raise.
While our hearts rebounding thrill
with joy which death alone can still.
Summer's heat or winter's cold
the seasons pass the years will roll.
Time and change will surely show
how firm thy friendship . . . O-HI-O!

© *Neal C. Lauron - USA TODAY NETWORK via Imagn Images*

Breaking The U

The Win That Ended a Hurricane Dynasty

T he nickname of the Miami Hurricanes football team is The U. It comes from the half orange/half green U-shaped logo displayed on their helmets. In the early 2000s, the image was intimidating. Year after year the Hurricanes team was packed with talent. They started to seem invincible. The 2001 Hurricanes squad had won the national championship, and in 2002 the team finished their regular season **undefeated**. This put them on a 34-game winning streak. That season, the Hurricanes starting roster included a whopping *eleven* future first-round NFL draft picks.

Ohio State's leading scorer was their kicker, Mike Nugent. Their season had been full of close games, yet the Buckeyes had managed to win all of them for a perfect 13-0 record. Head coach Jim Tressel did not quite carry Miami's swagger. Even so, his team had rightfully earned their spot in the Fiesta Bowl National Championship against the herculean Hurricanes. Most doubted they would be able to play up to the skill and speed of Miami. The 'Canes were favored to win by more than 10 points.

The game was played 1,000 miles away from Ohio Stadium in Tempe, Arizona. As fans filed into their seats, a sea of scarlet and gray faithful washed over the stadium. The place began to look and sound like a home game at the Horseshoe—a definite spark for the Buckeyes. The battle began. Despite all the talk about how good Miami was, it was Ohio State that led 14-7 at halftime.

Midway through the third quarter, the Buckeyes were 6 yards shy of another touchdown. Quarterback Craig Krenzel locked eyes on an open

Fact Blitz!

In the 2003 Fiesta Bowl Championship game, 37 of the 43 starters were drafted to play in the NFL with 14 of them becoming first-round draft picks. Why only 43 starters instead of 44? Ohio State junior Chris Gamble started as both a wide receiver on offense and a cornerback on defense!

receiver, but Miami defensive back Sean Taylor was one step ahead of him. Taylor intercepted the pass and raced back toward Ohio State's end zone. Fans gasped as he sliced through the Buckeye offense and saw open field ahead. The only player that stood between him and a touchdown was Buckeyes running back Maurice Clarett.

Running backs don't do much tackling, but Clarett read the play immediately. The freshman tracked Taylor down and stripped the ball right out of his hands! A second **turnover** in the same play! Shortly after, the Buckeyes kicked a field goal to give them a 17-7 lead.

A fourth-quarter Hurricane touchdown cut Ohio State's lead down to 17-14. With little time remaining, Ohio State had the ball. A first down meant they could run the clock out to win the game. Krenzel threw a pass to wide receiver Chris Gamble, who made a spectacular diving catch while dragging his foot as he fell out-of-bounds. It looked like a first down!

Unfortunately, the official signaled that Gamble was out-of-bounds when he caught it and so the pass didn't count. Replays later showed this call was incorrect, but in 2003, officials couldn't review plays on video screens the way they can today. The call stood and the Buckeyes were forced to punt the ball back to Miami.

Buckeye fans watched with heavy hearts as Miami returned Ohio State's punt all the way back to their own 26-yard line. Their kicker easily scored the 40-yard field goal to tie the score, 17-17. The Hurricanes were still alive and well. The battle would go into overtime.

Miami's mojo was back. They got the ball first and scored a touchdown in just five plays. One stop would win them the game. Again and again, the Buckeyes tried to score, only to come up short. On fourth down, Krenzel threw and missed Gamble on a high, incomplete pass. Ohio State fans hung their heads. It seemed the magical ride had come to an end. Miami players stormed the field as fireworks exploded overhead for a 'Canes victory. The celebration was in full swing when a small yellow penalty flag was spotted lying in the end zone. **Pass interference** had been called on the Miami defender! The swarm of people gathering on the field had to be cleared out and Ohio State set up with a fresh set of downs. Three plays later Krenzel ran in for a touchdown, tying the game 24-24. The game marched into a *second* overtime.

This time it was the Buckeyes who scored a quick touchdown, making the score 31-24. Miami needed a touchdown to stay in the game. They drove down to the 2-yard line. It quickly became 4th down for Miami. The Buckeye defenders seemed to form a stone wall as they lined up in front of their end zone. Linebacker Cie Grant blitzed quarterback Ken Dorsey on the snap. Later, Grant told Sports Illustrated, "When I lined up and saw there was no tight end in front of me, I knew the game was over." Dorsey's jolted pass sailed lifelessly through the air and fell short of the end zone. They had done it! The Buckeyes had just declared themselves the 2003 National Champions!

The mighty Buckeyes broke The U that night when they took down the Hurricanes—a team few believed could be beaten. There have been many unforgettable games over the years, but none of them quite capture the magic of that warm January night in Arizona when the Buckeyes proved to the world that they were national champions.

© AP Photo/Mark J. Terrill

*Quarterback Craig Krenzel signals his touchdown sending the 2003
Fiesta Bowl into a second overtime*

2003 Fiesta Bowl Championship Game Starters Selected for the NFL Draft

Ohio State Buckeyes®

Will Smith (2004, round 1)
Chris Gamble (2004, round 1)
Michael Jenkins (2004, round 1)
Michael Doss (2003, round 2)
Cie Grant (2003, round 3)
Darrion Scott (2004, round 3)
Kenny Peterson (2004, round 3)
Tim Anderson (2004, round 3)
Ben Hartsock (2004, round 3)
Dustin Fox (2005, round 3)
Maurice Clarett (2005, round 3)
Matt Wilhelm (2003, round 4)
Alex Stepanovich (2004, round 4)
Donnie Nickey (2003, round 5)
Craig Krenzel (2004, round 5)
Robert Reynolds (2004, round 5)
Adrien Clarke (2004, round 7)
Shane Olivea (2004, round 7)

2003 Fiesta Bowl Championship Game Starters Selected for the NFL Draft

Miami Hurricanes

Willis McGahee (2003 round 1)
Andre Johnson (2003, round 1)
William Joseph (2003, round 1)
Jerome McDougle (2003, round 1)
Sean Taylor (2004, round 1)
Kellen Winslow II (2004, round 1)
Jonathan Vilma (2004, round 1)
D.J. Williams (2004, round 1)
Vernon Carey (2004, round 1)
Antrel Rolle (2005, round 1)
Kelly Jennings (2006, round 1)
Roscoe Parrish (2005, round 2)
Roger McIntosh (2006, round 2)
Jamaal Green (2003, round 4)
Matt Walters (2003, round 5)
Chris Myers (2005, round 6)
Ken Dorsey (2003, round 7)
Carlos Joseph (2004, round 7)

 # Keys to the Game!

undefeated – a team that has not lost a game in a particular season.

turnover – when a team loses possession of the ball to the other team during a play—usually a fumble or an interception.

pass interference – when a defensive player illegally hinders the ability of the receiver to catch a pass.

Because I Couldn't Go For 3

A Legend of Woody Hayes

The most important game every year for the Buckeyes is their last one of the season against the Michigan Wolverines. In 1968,

Ohio State was 8-0 heading into this monster matchup. However, the maize and blue (Michigan's colors) were on a winning streak themselves. They had won seven games in a row and the only team standing between the Buckeyes and a perfect season.

Ohio State's head coach that year was a man named Woody Hayes. He reigned as the team's leader for 27 seasons from 1951-1978. No one despised Michigan more than Hayes. The game was going to be a tough battle.

Michigan struck first, driving 80 yards for a touchdown and a 7-0 lead. As halftime drew near, the score was tied 14-14. What seemed at first to be

Fact Blitz!

Because of the importance of the game to both teams, the rivalry matchup between Ohio State and Michigan is referred to simply as "The Game."

a close game did not last. Right before the half, the Buckeyes scored again, and after halftime they obliterated the Wolverines. They scored a whopping four more touchdowns and tacked on a field goal. Ohio State was now leading with a score of 50-14. Nothing satisfied coach Woody Hayes like a resounding victory over Michigan.

Then a peculiar thing happened. After the last touchdown, Coach Hayes sent his offense back onto the field to go for a ***2-point conversion***, rather than trying the traditional extra point kick. Hayes' grasp for an even bigger lead this late in the game made Michigan players, coaches, and fans furious. The Buckeyes failed to complete that extra 2-point conversion, and the game ended with a final score of 50-14. The story has it that when asked why he went for 2 points instead of 1, Hayes shot back, "*because I couldn't go for 3!*" The quote has been a beloved part of Buckeye legend ever since.

There is a mystery behind this legend: Hayes may not have actually said it! Many claim they heard Woody say it at one time or another, but no record exists of him giving this quote to any reporter after the game. He explained afterwards that the reason he couldn't kick the usual extra point was because both of his kickers were injured. He also admitted "they wanted more than 50 points." But did Woody Hayes say these famous words?

What we know is that no head coach in Ohio State history did more to fan the flames of the rivalry

Fact Blitz!

The bad blood between Michigan and Ohio State dates back a long time. In 1835, the state of Ohio and state of Michigan fought in the Toledo War over a small piece of land at their border. President Andrew Jackson settled that dispute by giving Ohio the land and Michigan the Upper Peninsula.

with the Michigan Wolverines than Woody Hayes. It was Woody who popularized the nickname "That Team Up North" rather than say the word "Michigan" out loud. According to legend, the team bus was once low on gas while driving home from Michigan's stadium, but Hayes declared that he would rather push the bus back to Ohio on foot than give the state of Michigan one cent of his money.

Seven seasons earlier, in 1961, the Buckeyes scored a touchdown to make the score 48-20 on the Wolverines with 6 seconds left. Many fans had already left the stadium when coach Hayes decided to again add insult to injury and go for 2 points, driving the final game score up 50-20. It seemed he did make a habit of running up the score on his rival when he could.

In the end, Hayes probably went for 2 that day because he didn't have a kicker, because they wanted more than 50 points, AND because he really would have gone for 3 points if he could have.

Whether the words were said in a locker-room moment right after the game, to one player, to another coach, or at some later time, the quote was attributed to Hayes. "Because I couldn't go for 3" is the kind of mindset Woody had when it came to "That Team Up North." Now, 50 years later it is still loved and spoken of by Ohio State fans. It's just how the famous coach would have wanted it.

In 1967, Woody Hayes walked the sideline in East Lansing in short sleeves and his familiar baseball cap, which collected snow through the afternoon

Woody Hayes: A Profile

Woody Hayes was a larger-than-life coach of the Buckeyes from 1951-1978. The first thing people usually remember about him is that he had a bad temper, and it got him into trouble. Most notably, he was ultimately fired for hitting a player in the 1978 Gator Bowl.

What is often forgotten is that Hayes had a much softer side. When he **recruited** a player, he talked more to them about their future in school than about their future on the football team. He would show up to visit hospital patients and tell them to keep his visit secret. He would pop into classes on campus simply to listen and learn. He loved winning football games but pushing people to be their absolute best was his passion.

Woody Hayes' famous coaching style was known as "three yards and a cloud of dust." He would not put up with silly mistakes and hated risky plays. His offense was simple: run 3 yards up the middle of the field. It wasn't flashy like a long pass, but when executed perfectly, it was almost impossible to stop. The idea was that running the football each time slowly wore the other team down . . . and it worked!

 # Keys to the Game!

2-point conversion – after a touchdown (6 points), there are two choices: kick the ball through the yellow goal posts (1 point) OR run/pass the ball into the end zone (2 points). Choosing to go for 2 points is more difficult and usually only used when the score of a game is close.

recruited – to be sought after by a coach who is looking for new players. A coach decides which players to pursue among high school athletes across the country. These selected athletes are then invited to go visit a school and offered incentives to come and play.

Coming Up Roses

*Joe Germaine's 1997 Game-Winning
Rose Bowl Drive*

In 1997, the Buckeyes were invited to play in the Rose Bowl for the first time in 12 years. The game would feature the Ohio State Buckeyes versus the Arizona State Sun Devils. The way both teams got to the big game, however, looked very different.

The last few years had been a tough go for the Buckeyes. They had lost six of their last seven bowl games. Their Heisman Trophy-winning running back, Eddie George, had moved to the NFL. Adding to the stress was a quarterback controversy. Stanley Jackson would be the Buckeyes starting quarterback, but Joe Germaine would also share time at the position. This dual quarterback system made it hard to tell who was leading the team. Worst of all, the Buckeyes were coming off a 13-9 loss to Michigan.

Meanwhile Arizona State had roared through their season unbeaten. By the time the Sun Devils were chosen for the bowl game, they were ranked No. 2 in the nation. The team was led by quarterback Jake "The Snake" Plummer, a Heisman Trophy finalist. If the team needed extra motivation to compete against Ohio State, they had it. Their former coach, John Cooper, was now Ohio State's head coach—it would be extra sweet to beat him! The Sun Devils and their fans were ready to prove they could take on Ohio State and win. The stadium was packed with 100,635 people to see how this game would unfold.

At the start of the fourth quarter, the Buckeyes were ahead 14-10. So, the Sun Devils

🏈 Huddle Up!

The Rose Bowl is the oldest of bowl games, dating all the way back to 1902. The 100-year-old stadium sits in the mountains of Southern California. It began as a matchup of the Big Ten champion against the Pac-10 champion (East versus West). It is always played on New Year's Day and is known as the "Granddaddy of Them All." Before the days of College Football Playoffs and computer ranking systems, playing in this game was one of Ohio State's biggest goals each year.

looked to their quarterback for leadership. He was nicknamed "The Snake" because he had a knack for slipping through tacklers to make big plays—and that's just what he did. Late in the fourth quarter, Plummer completed a pass on a fourth down. Then, with less than two minutes left in the game, he slid away from the Buckeye defenders for an 11-yard touchdown run, sending Sun Devil fans into a frenzy and Ohio State fans into despair. Arizona State was ahead 17-14 with only 1:33 left to play.

Buckeye fans needed a miracle and wondered which quarterback could produce one. Joe Germaine's name was called. He jogged to the field and took command of the huddle. What followed was one of the biggest comeback drives in Ohio State history.

Germaine connected with Dimitrious Stanley for three critical first downs keeping the Buckeyes drive alive. He tried to find Stanley again, but the play drew a pass interference call against the Sun Devils. A second pass interference call on a pass intended for David Boston put the Buckeyes at a first-and-goal with 24 seconds left. The play-call was *Two-Left Twins, 240 Smash.* Germaine took the snap and scanned for an open receiver. David Boston faked his man inside and drifted back out.

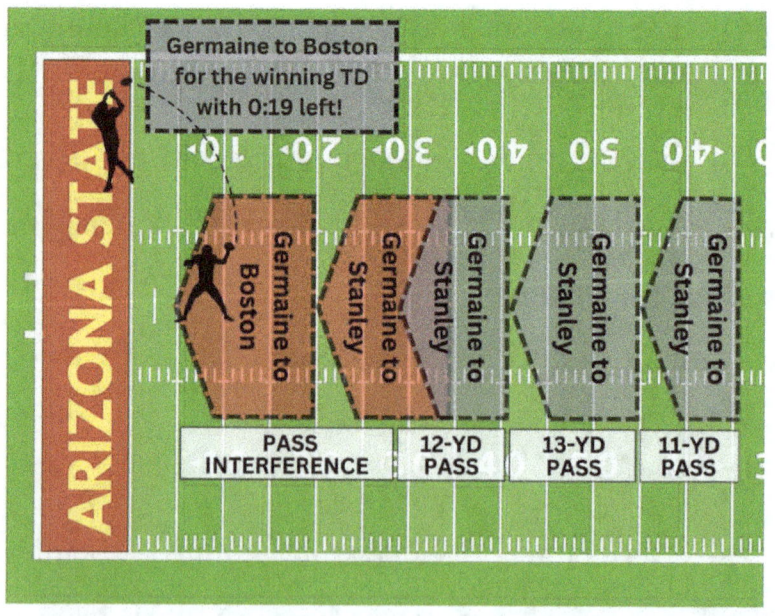

Key Plays in the drive to win the 1997 Rose Bowl

The ball sailed across the field and into his hands. There were no defenders around Boston as he walked untouched into the end zone and added a little strut for show. Germaine not only led his team down the field with precision passing—he made it look good!

Sun Devil fans were in shock. A blocked extra point wasn't enough. The Buckeyes zipped up a final score of 20-17 and Ohio State won the game!

It was Ohio State's first Rose Bowl victory in 23 years and the peak of head coach Cooper's career. The win boosted Ohio State to No. 2 in the country—their highest ranking since 1973. "That victory was for Columbus!" Cooper exclaimed on the field after the powerful Rose Bowl victory.

The Buckeyes certainly "rose" to the occasion that day!

David Boston runs into the end zone for the winning touchdown at the Rose Bowl as #3 Dimitrious Stanley jumps for joy

Time Out for Tradition

Brutus Buckeye®

Brutus Buckeye is the official mascot for The Ohio State University. His school spirit is contagious when he pumps up a crowd, performs backflips and rigorously pounds his large head between his fists. Today, he dons a scarlet and gray striped shirt, 'Block O' baseball cap, and football gloves. His enormous, friendly, oversized head is shaped like an actual Buckeye nut. Brutus began as a paper mâché ball back in 1965. Although his look has changed over the years, he has faithfully cheered on the Buckeyes ever since.

Time Out for Tradition

Brutus Buckeye

1965

1979

1981

1986

© The Ohio State University Archives

A Picture Worth a Thousand Words

Eddie George vs. Notre Dame

T he Ohio State Buckeyes and the Notre Dame Fighting Irish are both powerhouse football programs. In 1995, they were set to play each other for the first time in 50 years. Fans were excited about the rare matchup. Both the Buckeyes and the Irish had started their seasons strong. Everyone was excited to find out who would win this big game.

A ticket to the game that year was $25. Once those sold out, people started paying hundreds of dollars per ticket for a chance to get into the Horseshoe. The stadium was packed with 95,537 people—a new record.

The game lived up to its hype. Midway through the fourth quarter, Ohio State had a 35-26 lead. There had been several highlight-reel moments from Buckeye players: Buckeyes quarterback Bobby Hoying had already thrown three magnificent touchdown passes. Then, Buckeye cornerback Shawn Springs intercepted a pass late in the third quarter. He grabbed the ball out of the air just as Notre Dame was about to score. Hoying then threw a pass to **All-American** receiver Terry Glenn who slipped between two Irish defenders and ran for an 82-yard touchdown!

After all that action, the Buckeyes just had to hold onto their lead. Running plays are the best way to do that because they keep the game clock moving, leaving less time for the other team to score. This meant the pressure was now on Ohio State's running back, Eddie George.

George was in the middle of a season where he would rush for 1,927 yards—a Buckeye record. When he finished his football career at Ohio State after four years, he was one of the program's best ever players. His jersey number 27, now retired, hangs in honor inside Ohio Stadium. He would eventually go on to play eight seasons in the NFL and rush for over 10,000 yards in his career.

Now, here he was on the field against Notre Dame. His job was to safely run the ball so that the

Eddie George breaking away from the Notre Dame defense for a 61-yard run

© Fred Squillante – USA TODAY NETWORK via Imagn Images

clock would run down to zero. George decided he could do better than that. As the Buckeye offense lined up, he found a hole and sliced through the Irish defense for a 61-yard run. The moment itself, captured by Columbus Dispatch photographer Fred Squillante, produced one of Ohio State's most iconic photographs. From Squillante's camera angle, George is pictured alone running away from not one but SEVEN helpless Notre Dame defenders.

He was finally knocked out of bounds three yards from the end zone. Three plays later, George punched it in himself to give the Buckeyes a 42-26 lead. Just like the Irish couldn't catch George in the historic picture, Notre Dame would not catch Ohio State that day. The final score of the game was 45-26, a triumphant Buckeyes victory!

George sped his way straight into the Ohio State history books. He ran for 207 yards in that game against Notre Dame. Then, later in the season, he had a whopping 314 rushing yards against Illinois! His performance that year earned him the Heisman Trophy, the highest award in college football. His run at Ohio State, just like the famous photograph, proved to be "picture perfect."

🏈 Huddle Up!

As a freshman in 1992, Eddie George started strong, but things took a bad turn for him in a game against Illinois. He fumbled the ball, which resulted in a 96-yard Illinois touchdown. Later that same game, he fumbled the ball *again*. Illinois recovered it and drove for the game-winning touchdown. His coaches didn't trust him after two such critical mistakes. It took almost two years of practice and hard work before they would give him significant playing time again. Head coach John Cooper described George as having tremendous focus and a better work ethic than any college player in football history. His decorated football career following his shaky start is certainly proof of that.

Keys to the Game!

All-American – a player selected as the best in the country at their specific position. Since 1929, a Buckeye tree has been planted in a place called "Buckeye Grove" to honor each OSU All-American football player. Buckeye Grove can be found in the southwest corner of the stadium.

© Photo credit: Keith J Finks / Shutterstock.com

Time Out for Tradition

Buckeye Leaf Helmet Stickers

A buckeye leaf is easy to spot. It is richly green in color with five single leaflets blossoming from its center. The leaves resemble the five fingers on your hand. They grow on Ohio's state tree, the buckeye tree, and represent strength and sturdiness.

In 1967, Woody Hayes began to give players a buckeye leaf sticker if they made an exceptional play on the field. The stickers could then be worn on helmets as small badges of honor. It was an idea that "stuck." From then on, Woody Hayes awarded buckeye leaf stickers each week to players who earned them.

The sticker itself is round, white, and about the size of a quarter. Each one, when earned, is carefully hand-placed on Buckeyes helmets throughout the season. As time goes on, players collect more and more. Each helmet can hold about 80-90 buckeye leaves.

This sticker system is a cherished Ohio State football tradition and is still used today, although the criteria for earning one has changed.

While Woody Hayes awarded them to individual players, coaches like Jim Tressel focused on awarding them to the whole team and the smaller units that make up the team. Since they first appeared on Buckeyes helmets back in 1967, many other colleges football teams have followed suit. For example, Clemson gives out paw print stickers, Georgia gives out dog bones and even Michigan now awards players with wolverine stickers. Each sticker represents a moment of exceptional performance.

Examples of how to earn a sticker:

Awarded to Individual
Score a touchdown
Cause a fumble or recovery
Kick a field goal over 45 yards

Awarded to a Small Group
No turnovers (offensive unit)
Score 24 points (offensive unit)
Opponent scores 13 points or less (defensive unit)

Awarded to Entire Team
1 sticker per win
2 stickers per conference win
3 stickers for a Michigan win

*No players are awarded a buckeye leaf sticker
following an Ohio State loss.

Ohio State Against the World

Jack Sawyer's Scoop-and-Score Launches Bucks to a National Championship

The stage was set for a resounding Buckeye victory. For three straight years Ohio State had lost their big rivalry game to

Michigan–but the Wolverines had also been accused of breaking rules by using stolen play signs during each of those victories. Buckeye fans were thirsty for revenge, and it looked like they were going to get it.

Going into the 2024 matchup against Michigan, Ohio State was ranked #2 in the country. Their roster was jam-packed with talent and the game would be played in Columbus on their home turf. Michigan, however, had stumbled to an unimpressive 6-5 record and two of their best players would be out due to injury. The Wolverines were predicted to lose by more than 20 points.

And then it began. Watching The Game that year as a Buckeye fan was like being trapped in a horrible nightmare with no way to wake up. Everything that could have gone wrong, did. The day was filled with missed field goals, dropped kickoff returns, interceptions, and silly penalties. Most frustratingly, the high-powered Buckeye offense seemed to run the ball into a wall of Michigan defenders play after play. The final scoreboard was not a dream: Michigan 13, Ohio State 10. The stunning loss, a fourth in a row to the Wolverines, cost the Buckeyes a chance to play for the Big Ten Championship.

To make matters worse, Ohio State team captain, Jack Sawyer, and several of his teammates were playing their final season for Ohio State. They had never beat Michigan–and now they never would. Anger and disappointment surrounded the team. While the

Fact Blitz!

Before 2021, college athletes were not allowed to make money on the sport they played. In 2021, NCAA rules changed so that players could make money on their Name, Image and Likeness (NIL). In 2025, Ohio State players earned over $20 million playing for the team!

devastating loss did not keep the Buckeyes out of the **College Football Playoff**, their path to the national championship was a hard one. Experts questioned whether the troubled team would play well.

Three days later, the Buckeyes held a meeting. They decided this was not how they would be remembered, and they were still determined to achieve something great.

Rallying from the Michigan rubble, that

appeared to be true. What looked like a new team emerged as the Bucks stormed through their first round playoff game, a 42-17 romp, never giving the Tennessee Volunteers a chance. The win sent them to the second round where they would face undefeated and #1 ranked Oregon in the Rose Bowl. That game would be a rematch after the Oregon Ducks beat Ohio State by 1 point earlier in the season.

Fans wondered which version of the Buckeyes would show up–the team that steamrolled Tennessee, or the one that fell flat against Michigan. To the delight of Ohio State fans, that question was answered when Ohio State jumped all over the Ducks, leading 34-0 in the first half before cruising to a 41-21 win.

After back-to-back domination in the first two playoff rounds, it was clear that Ohio State was the team to beat. Four teams remained. The Bucks were off to the semifinals to face the Texas Longhorns. The winner would advance to the National Championship game.

It was an unusually cold day in Dallas but the stadium was charged with excitement. Unlike the previous two games, every time Ohio State scored a touchdown, Texas would answer right back with one of their own.

With 4 minutes left to play in the fourth quarter, it was 21-14 Buckeyes. Texas was deep in Buckeye territory. With a first-and-goal and only 1 yard to go, they were perfectly positioned to tie the game. The Ohio State defense lined up determined to defend that final yard with a ***goal line stand***.

On first down, the Buckeye defense stuffed Texas running back Jerrick Gibson just short of the goal line for no gain. On second down, Buckeye safety Lathan Ransom tracked down Texas running back Quintrevion Wisner and tackled him in the backfield for a huge 7-yard loss. Texas was rattled. On third down, the Ohio State defense pressured Texas quarterback Quinn Ewers into a quick throw. His pass sailed to the corner of the end zone where it fell incomplete.

It was now fourth-and-goal for Texas. Down 7 points and with only two minutes remaining, the Longhorns had to go for the touchdown. One more stop by the Ohio State defense would win the game for the Buckeyes. The teams lined up and the ball was snapped. Rushing around the Texas offensive line, Sawyer broke free. He began closing in on Ewers. With a swing of his mighty arm, Sawyer struck from behind. The ball was jarred loose from the impact of his hit–a fumble! As if the ball had the name "Jack Sawyer" stamped on it, it bounced once on the turf and right back up into his arms. He scooped it up and began sprinting back down the field! Head coach Ryan Day took off down the sideline after him jumping and shouting. 83-yards later, "Captain Jack" crossed into the end zone for a touchdown that sent Buckeye players and fans into a frenzy. Jack Sawyer's **scoop-and-score** sealed the victory, putting the Buckeyes up 28-14. The game was now out of reach for Texas.

© Adam Cairns - USA TODAY NETWORK via Imagn Images

Texas quarterback Quinn Ewers' fumble bounces right into Jack Sawyer's hands during Ohio State's semifinal win

As Ohio State quarterback Will Howard took a knee to run the clock out, coach Day could not contain his excitement. He ran over and jumped into Jack Sawyer's arms. The moment was heartwarming. After the game Day told reporters, "To make a play like that, in that moment... You want to leave a legacy behind? You become a legend. He [Sawyer] just became a legend at Ohio State." The Buckeyes beat Texas with a final score of 28-14. It was a historic win and one that punched their ticket to the National Championship.

Ten days later, the Buckeyes finished the job. They beat Notre Dame 31-23 to capture the National Championship! Silver and gold confetti poured down from the rafters. Players lifted the

Fact Blitz!

Earlier in their college careers, Ohio State defensive lineman Jack Sawyer and Texas quarterback Quinn Ewers were roommates and teammates at Ohio State. Ewers left Ohio State after one season to play for Texas.

trophy into the air. That same team that sat together in despair after Michigan, now celebrated together on top of the world—as champions!

Ohio State players celebrate after defeating Notre Dame to become the champions of college football for the 2024-2025 season

 # Keys to the Game!

College Football Playoff (CFP) – A tournament where the best teams are selected to play with the winner being crowned the national champion. In 2024, the CFP was expanded to include the best 12 teams.

goal line stand – when a defense manages to stop an offense from scoring a touchdown within 10 yards of the end zone. The opposing team is so close, that the defensive players line up on their own goal line, or even in their own end zone!

scoop-and-score – a play made by the defense when a player picks up (scoops up) a fumble from the ground and then runs back into the opposite end zone for a touchdown (a score).

More Shining Moments from the 2024-2025 Playoff Sweep

Second Round vs. Oregon: Star freshman wide receiver Jeremiah Smith caught a 45-yard touchdown pass less than a minute into the game. He had another 43-yard touchdown catch in the second quarter to put the Buckeyes up by 24 points. He was named offensive MVP of the game.

Semifinals vs. Texas: Just before halftime, Texas had just tied the game 7-7. The tie lasted only 16 seconds. With 28 seconds left on the clock, running back TreVeyon Henderson caught a short screen pass and turned it up the field for a thrilling (and game-changing) 75-yard touchdown.

National Championship Game vs. Notre Dame: Quarterback Will Howard had a nearly perfect first half. He completed 14/15 passes for 144 yards, had two touchdowns, no turnovers, and 26 rushing yards. He set the record for consecutive passes completed in a championship game and was named offensive MVP of the game.

Continued on next page →

In the final minutes of the game, Howard threw a sensational 56-yard pass on third down that landed in the hands of Smith. The monster play set up a field goal that put the Buckeyes up 34-23 and drove the game out of reach for the Irish.

The G.O.A.T.

Archie Griffin Plays as a Freshman

A football player has four seasons of eligibility when they enroll at Ohio State. (A *freshman* is year one, a *sophomore* is year two, a *junior* is year three, and a *senior* is year four.) Up until 1972, NCAA rules stated that freshmen football players could practice with the team but couldn't play in games. That rule changed in 1972, and it was good timing for Ohio State. That year they had recruited a player named Archie Griffin.

Even with the rule change, most freshmen weren't good enough yet to play in games, so it was surprising to see Griffin trot onto the field for the first game of the season. His very first play ended with a fumble and a 5-yard loss. Coach Woody Hayes must have seen something in the young running back though, because the following week he started him again against the North Carolina Tar Heels. This time, Archie did better—a LOT better. By the end of the game, a 29-14 Buckeyes victory, Griffin had run for a monstrous 239 yards. His single-game rushing yards broke a 27-year-old team record! After the game, the North Carolina head coach, Bill Dooley, admitted to reporters, "we didn't know that Griffin existed." Griffin, the freshman, had proved he was the right running back for the job.

© *The Ohio State University Archives*

Archie Griffin runs the football against North Carolina in 1972

The Buckeyes fought their way to an 8-1 record that season with Griffin running for over 800 yards. People started to notice. "I've never been for or against the freshmen rule, but Archie has made me change my mind," Hayes remarked to reporters. Griffin's final game as a freshman was against Ohio State's longtime rival, Michigan. The Wolverines had a powerhouse team that year—they were undefeated, with a No. 3 national ranking and heavily favored to win. After a low-scoring first half, Griffin ran 17 yards to set up a first-and-goal and then rushed for the first Buckeye touchdown of the game, to make the score 7-3. Following a 35-yard run from QB Greg Hare early in the third quarter, Griffin took a handoff up the middle, suddenly broke right, then sprinted to the end zone for an explosive 30-yard touchdown.

Rolls of paper streamed down from the stands at Ohio Stadium in celebration. The sensational dash gave the Buckeyes a solid 14-3 lead. They went on to *upset* Michigan that day 14-11. The triumphant victory ended Michigan's 15-game winning streak, crushed their hopes of a national championship, and handed them their first regular-season loss in two years. The Wolverines faced Griffin and the Buckeyes three more times over the next three years. Each time, Michigan came in undefeated. Each time they never managed to pull out a win. Michigan's coach Bo Schembechler later said of Griffin, "I swear in four years, we never tackled the guy."

Archie Griffin went on to win the Heisman Trophy his junior year in 1974 and then again his senior year in 1975. He is the only football player so far in history to have won the trophy twice. Not many people can think of Ohio State football without thinking of Griffin. By the end of his senior season, no one had rushed for more yards in a college career. Archie Griffin, the true "freshman" who had trotted onto the field in 1972, certainly had a lot to be proud of. His jersey number, 45, hangs retired in honor at Ohio Stadium.

© AP Photo/File

Archie Griffin holds up two fingers as he poses with the Heisman Trophy after being named the winner for the second time in a row – the only player in history to have won it twice

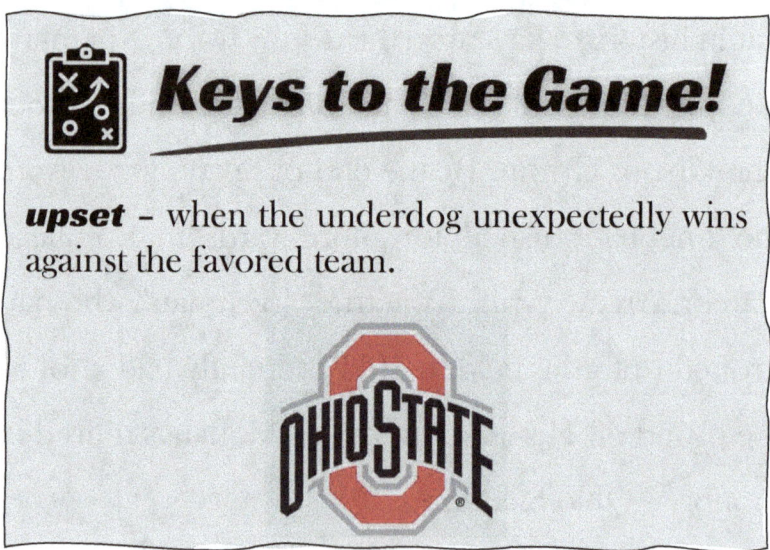

Keys to the Game!

upset – when the underdog unexpectedly wins against the favored team.

Time Out for Tradition

Heisman Trophy Winners

The Heisman Memorial Trophy is a prestigious award given once a year to the most outstanding player in college football. It has been awarded every year since 1935. The trophy is made from a very heavy cast bronze. It is 13.5 inches tall, 14 inches long, 16 inches wide and weighs about 45 pounds (about as heavy as four bowling balls!) Here are Ohio State's Heisman Trophy Winners over the years:

1944 - Les Horvath
1950 - Vic Janowicz
1955 - Howard "Hopalong" Cassady
1974 - Archie Griffin
1975 - Archie Griffin
1995 - Eddie George
2006 - Troy Smith

A Lost Shoe in the 'Shoe

Keith Byars Seals the Comeback Against Illinois

Perhaps the most unique trophy in college football is a carved wooden turtle named Illibuck. The tradition started back in

1925 with a live turtle symbolizing the hopeful long life of the rivalry between Ohio State and Illinois. There was one problem: turtles don't live as long as rivalries! After his passing, the schools decided it would be better to make a wooden replica of the turtle. The winner of the Ohio State Buckeyes/Illinois Fighting Illini game has received that trophy ever since.

© Photo by Scott W. Grau/Icon Sportswire via AP Images

Ohio State quarterback J.T. Barrett holding the carved wooden Illibuck Trophy in the rain after beating Illinois 52-14 on 11/18/2017

Going into the 1984 game, Illibuck was in the hands of the Fighting Illini. It was a beautiful day in Columbus for the No. 8 ranked Buckeyes, but Illinois stormed into the Horseshoe intending to ruin it. After three touchdown passes and a field goal, the Illini took a gigantic 24-0 lead just two plays into the second quarter. It wasn't even halftime, and many fans were already heading for the exits.

Keith Byars was the Buckeyes leading tailback that year under head coach Earle Bruce. Unlike the 90,000 fans in attendance, Byars didn't seem rattled by the scoreboard. With his team down 24 points, he made a cool 16-yard touchdown run to put Ohio State on the board. The cheers from the crowd sounded more relieved than excited, but the score seemed to boost the beleaguered Buckeyes' confidence.

Coach Bruce then called for a surprise **onside kick**. To the shock of everyone, the

Buckeyes recovered it! Ohio State quarterback Mike Tomczak then faked a handoff and threw the ball high in the air. Wide receiver Cris Carter leapt over three defenders, caught the ball, and fell into the end zone—touchdown Buckeyes! The score was now 24-14 and it wasn't even halftime. After a Buckeyes interception, Byars ran in his second touchdown of the day, sending the score to 24-21 at the half. Ohio State was right back in it.

Byars seemed unstoppable. He ran for yet *another* touchdown early in the third quarter giving the Buckeyes their first lead of the game. Thunderous cheers filled the stadium, but they didn't last long. Illinois added a field goal to stay right on the Buckeyes' heels 28-27.

Up by only one point, the Buckeyes began a drive from their own 33-yard line—and Byars was about to make a play that would instantly become the highlight of his college career.

Fact Blitz!

The Big Ten Conference is often written as B1G. The 1 is both a one in the number 10 and an *i* in the word *big*. Likewise, the *G* is both a *g* in the word *big* and *zero* in the number 10.

Taking a snap, Tomczak handed the ball to Byars, who ran through a big hole on the right side. With Illini defenders closing in for the tackle, Byars made a sharp move to the middle. As he cut back, his left shoe came loose. Byars made a split-second decision. Fans watched wide-eyed as Byars kicked his shoe seamlessly off his foot—without breaking stride—and sprinted the last 41 yards of his run to the end zone in just his sock! He had just outrun five Illinois defenders with only one shoe on! "I felt the shoe slip, and it just popped off," Byars said after the game. "I wasn't about to slow down to go back and get it. I tried to get to the end zone as quick as

possible and hope no one would step on my size 14."
Keith Byars' foot (a shoe size of 14) is about as long
as a 2-liter bottle of soda! The shoeless touchdown
run and extra point that followed put Ohio State up
35-27.

Ohio State fans were in a frenzy, but Illinois
wasn't ready to hand the Illibuck Trophy over quite
yet. Their quarterback Jack Trudeau answered with
his fourth touchdown pass of the day, followed by a
2-point conversion to tie the game. After trading field
goals, the score was tied 38-38 late in the fourth
quarter and Ohio State had the ball.

Keith Byars still had some magic in his legs.
With just 36 seconds left in the game, and both
shoes back on, he ran left, then cut back right over
the left tackle for the go-ahead touchdown. It was his
fifth of the day! It not only won the game for the
Buckeyes, but it gave Byars an astounding 274
rushing yards. That was a new school record for a

single game, beating Archie Griffin's 246 yards against Iowa in 1973.

Byars' lost shoe in the 'Shoe came during one of Ohio State's most memorable comeback wins. The Buckeyes won the game that day 45-38 and went on to clinch the Big Ten title, earning a trip to the Rose Bowl. Keith Byars was voted runner-up for the Heisman Trophy that year and the most valuable player in the Big Ten Conference. The Illibuck Trophy was back with Ohio State and Byars had given fans a moment they wouldn't soon forget.

In 1984, Ohio State running back Keith Byars beat Illinois with only one shoe on

 **Keys to the Game!**

onside kick – an onside kick in college football is a short kickoff where the kicking team tries to regain possession of the ball. If the ball makes it 10 yards down the field, either team can recover it. These high-risk kicks are usually called when a game is close, and the kicking team badly needs the ball back.

The Call That Stood

J.T. Barrett Battles Michigan in Double Overtime

O ver 17 million people tuned in to watch the Ohio State versus Michigan game in 2016. The instant classic came with high stakes, emotional swings and a big controversial finish. Today, it is just as equally celebrated by Buckeye fans as it is protested by Michigan fans. The No. 2 Buckeyes battled the No. 3 Wolverines in a game that featured not one, but two overtimes. The thrill-packed finish hung on a single call by the officials that is analyzed and debated to this very day.

Urban Meyer entered his fifth season as head coach of the Buckeyes in 2016. He was undefeated against the Wolverines. Michigan coach Jim

Fact Blitz!

During the week leading up to the Ohio State/Michigan game, the letter X replaces the letter M in every single word on Ohio State's campus. Mirror Lake becomes Xirror Lake. Signs around campus say things like "15 Xinute parking" and "Xorrill Tower." Social media accounts are filled with phrases like, "Beat Xichigan!" The flurry of X's pump up school spirit on campus for "The GaXe."

Harbaugh, however, had a team that meant business. Earlier in the season they had beaten Rutgers 78-0. The Wolverines entered the game with a 10-1 record and a chance to play for the national championship if they could take down the Buckeyes.

The first quarter was a defensive tug-of-war. Both teams fought for control. Ohio State made one drive into Michigan territory, but Buckeye kicker Tyler Durbin missed a 37-yard field goal, leaving the first quarter scoreless.

After Michigan kicked a field goal early in the second quarter, Ohio State's safety Malik Hooker answered with an interception that he returned 16 yards for a touchdown. That put the Bucks on top, but not for long. The Wolverines scored again and led 10-7 going into halftime. Michigan began to pull away in the third quarter, increasing their lead to 17-7. Buckeye fans were frustrated. Ohio State had seen great success against Michigan the past four years. Now the maize and blue were ahead by 10.

A Buckeyes interception and touchdown made the score 17-14 with the Wolverines still ahead. Ohio State's best chance to tie the game came midway through the fourth quarter. Ohio State drove the ball all the way down to the Michigan 2-yard line—6 short feet from a touchdown to go ahead. Despite his missed kick earlier in the game, the team was depending on Durbin to make this field goal and tie the game. The ball was snapped, the kick was up, and everyone watched in horror as the ball hooked just left of the goal post—no good! The television cameras panned to a stunned Urban Meyer. His perfect record against Michigan looked like it was about to end.

On any good team, when one player stumbles, the rest of the team tries to pick him up. That's just what the Buckeyes did. First, the defense forced a **three-and-out**. Then, quarterback J.T. Barrett led a 13-play drive to the Michigan 5-yard line before calling a timeout with just 6 seconds left. Durbin was up again. Fans held their breath as he trotted out to attempt a critical field goal. This time, his aim was perfect. He sent the ball straight through the yellow posts for a successful 23-yard field goal! The clock ran out and the score was an even 17-17.

In overtime, each team would get a chance to score from the 25-yard line. Ohio State went first and scored a touchdown in two quick plays. All they had to do now was stop Michigan from scoring. The Wolverine drive came down to a fourth-and-goal from the 5-yard line. The Horseshoe roared in support, knowing that the Buckeye defense was one stop away from victory. Unfortunately, Michigan's quarterback found a receiver in the end zone for a touchdown. The score was tied again. The game was now headed to a *second* overtime.

This time Michigan got the ball first. They couldn't get close enough for a touchdown and had to settle for a field goal, putting the team up by 3 points (27-24). The Buckeyes had to answer back. It quickly became third down. Barrett handed the ball off to halfback Curtis Samuel. He was nearly tackled for a loss but zigzagged all the way back across the field to gain 8 yards—just 1 yard short of the first down. That's when things got interesting.

A field goal would result in another tie. Urban Meyer, under pressure, decided to go for it on fourth-and-1. If they couldn't gain a yard, they'd lose. The Buckeyes took their positions on the **line of scrimmage**. The ball was snapped to Barrett, and he charged forward. He crashed into a Michigan defender and then was knocked into his own tight end A.J. Alexander. Barrett appeared to reach the yellow first-down line but an instant later the collision knocked him backward at least a foot.

Ohio State Buckeye quarterback J.T. Barrett (16) gains a first down that was upheld by video review during a second overtime against Michigan

Michigan coach Harbaugh began frantically signaling with his arms that Barrett was tackled short of the first down. Even Barrett admitted later that he was unsure when he was tackled. The official ran over and marked the spot. Buckeye fans cheered when he signaled a first down. It was so close though that the officials needed to take another look on video. If Barrett was ruled short of the first down, the game was over. After a brief deliberation the official announcement filled the stadium: "*After review, the play stands as called on the field, first down.*" Buckeye fans erupted in cheers while Michigan fans stood shocked in disbelief. Multiple camera angles confirmed the first down, but only by a few inches.

The call lit a fire under the Buckeye offense. On the next play, Curtis Samuel took the ball and sliced through the Michigan defense. He sprinted 15 yards untouched and crossed the end zone with outstretched arms to score the winning touchdown! Ohio State fans stormed the field in celebration. After all that drama, their beloved Buckeyes had emerged victorious.

Emotions afterwards ran high on both sides. Urban Meyer was so overcome with happiness that he immediately threw himself face down on the field. "That was not a first down," Michigan coach Harbaugh said after the game. "I'm bitterly disappointed with the officiating today." The spot of the ball was analyzed and replayed for days after the game ended, but Ohio State got their fifth straight win over the Wolverines.

The 2016 Game had it all—fierce competition, struggle on both sides, nonstop shifts in momentum, two overtimes, and one incredibly close fourth down. It sent fans of both teams on an emotional roller-coaster ride from start to finish. In that spectacular game, the Buckeyes came out on top—if only by an inch.

Ohio State Curtis Samuel leaps into the end zone during the second overtime of Ohio State's 30-27 win over Michigan in 2016

© *Eric Seals - USA TODAY NETWORK via Imagn Images*

 # Keys to the Game!

three-and-out – when the offensive team runs their first three plays in a possession without gaining 10 yards for a first down and is forced to use their last down to punt the ball away.

line of scrimmage – an imaginary line (across the wide part of the field) that both teams cannot cross until the ball is snapped. It runs through the very tip of where the ball is placed on the field following the previous play.

© Kirby Lee - Imagn Images

Time Out for Tradition

History of the Gold Pants Club

The Buckeyes play an average of 12 games in their season against different opponents. A rival, however, is more than just an opponent. A rival is an *enemy*. A rivalry is caused by something that creates bad blood between two teams. The rivalry between the Ohio State Buckeyes and the Michigan Wolverines dates back over a century. These two teams met for the first time on October 16, 1897. From that first meeting until 1933, Michigan dominated the field with 24 wins and two ties out of 30 games.

Francis Schmidt became the head coach of the Buckeyes in 1934. One of the first questions he got from reporters was "How do you think your team will do against Michigan?" Schmidt, not phased at all by the Michigan football force, replied, "They put their pants on one leg at a time, same as everybody else." His cavalier attitude towards the Wolverines that day sparked a change. Michigan players should not be feared. They were not invincible. They were simply . . . regular people.

Upon hearing this, local businessman Simon Lazarus (president of Lazarus department stores) decided to form what is known today as, "The Gold Pants Club." He had gold charms made, each in the shape of a pair of football pants. Any player or coach on the Ohio State Buckeyes team would get one for beating Michigan. The charms would be etched with the player's or coach's initials, the date of victory and the score of the game.

In his first year as head coach (and following his famous quote), Schmidt led the team to a 34-0 shutout against the Wolverines. The shutouts continued for three straight years. Beating "That Team Up North" is very important to every Ohio State player each year, and the tradition and the Gold Pants Club lives on to this very day.

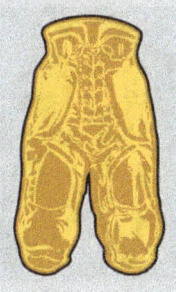

Ohio State vs. Michigan History

Year	Winning Team		Losing Team	
1897	MICHIGAN	34	OHIO STATE	0
1900	TIE	0	TIE	0
1901	MICHIGAN	21	OHIO STATE	0
1902	MICHIGAN	86	OHIO STATE	0
1903	MICHIGAN	36	OHIO STATE	0
1904	MICHIGAN	31	OHIO STATE	6
1905	MICHIGAN	40	OHIO STATE	0
1906	MICHIGAN	6	OHIO STATE	0
1907	MICHIGAN	22	OHIO STATE	0
1908	MICHIGAN	10	OHIO STATE	6
1909	MICHIGAN	33	OHIO STATE	6
1910	TIE	3	OHIO STATE	3
1911	MICHIGAN	19	OHIO STATE	0
1912	MICHIGAN	14	OHIO STATE	0
1918	MICHIGAN	14	OHIO STATE	0
1919	OHIO STATE	13	MICHIGAN	3
1920	OHIO STATE	14	MICHIGAN	7
1921	OHIO STATE	14	MICHIGAN	0
1922	MICHIGAN	19	OHIO STATE	0
1923	MICHIGAN	23	OHIO STATE	0
1924	MICHIGAN	16	OHIO STATE	6
1925	MICHIGAN	10	OHIO STATE	0
1926	MICHIGAN	17	OHIO STATE	16
1927	MICHIGAN	21	OHIO STATE	0
1928	OHIO STATE	19	MICHIGAN	7
1929	OHIO STATE	7	MICHIGAN	0
1930	MICHIGAN	13	OHIO STATE	0
1931	OHIO STATE	20	MICHIGAN	7
1932	MICHIGAN	14	OHIO STATE	0
1933	MICHIGAN	13	OHIO STATE	0
*1934	OHIO STATE	34	MICHIGAN	0
*1935	OHIO STATE	38	MICHIGAN	0
*1936	OHIO STATE	21	MICHIGAN	0
*1937	OHIO STATE	21	MICHIGAN	0

*Francis Schmidt's first four years as head coach of the Buckeyes

EARLE

Beating Michigan for Coach Bruce

I n 1950, a man named Earle Bruce was recruited to play fullback for Ohio State. Unfortunately, he hurt his knee during practice one day, and the injury ended his career. Bruce wasn't finished with football though. Perhaps he couldn't play, but he could still coach! He spent the next 28 years coaching high school and college football teams. He was great at it! Every team he coached seemed to win. In 1979, Ohio State had just fired head coach Woody Hayes. They needed a new coach and looked to that injured fullback from years ago.

In his first year as head coach, Bruce led the Buckeyes to an undefeated season. Hiring Bruce had been a win! Over eight seasons at Ohio State, Bruce won 75 games and lost only 22.

Things took a bad turn in his ninth season though. Wide receiver Cris Carter was supposed to be one of the Buckeyes' best players in 1987, but news broke that he was ruled ineligible to play. Morale dropped and the rest of the team struggled. The Indiana Hoosiers, who had not beaten Ohio

State in 38 years, came in and pounded the Bucks 31-10 in the Horseshoe. Ohio State then lost three games in a row leading up to the season-ending game against Michigan. Ohio State President Edward Jennings had had enough. He abruptly fired Bruce just days before the Michigan game.

Bruce, however, was loved by his team. His boss, athletic director Rick Bay, quit his job rather than tell Bruce about President Jennings' decision to fire him. Bay called it a "dark day" for Ohio State. Even though Jennings had fired Bruce, Ohio State said they would allow him to coach the final game against Michigan. The slight gesture had little impact. Instead of a week filled with spirit and school pride, everything now felt dark and sad. No one was quite sure what to expect from the bruised and broken-hearted Buckeyes as the Michigan game loomed ahead.

Bruce came out to coach his last game against

Michigan dressed in his usual outfit: a charcoal suit and fedora. Then it was time for the players to take the field. Fans were surprised when every Ohio State player jogged onto the field sporting a white headband with the name EARLE written across the front in red capital letters. It seemed that the team was motivated to win one more game for their beloved coach. At first Bruce wondered what was going on. He was just about to tell them to take the headbands off when he caught sight of what they said.

The heartfelt gesture did not have an immediate effect. In fact, the game started badly for Ohio State. In front of a jeering Wolverine crowd, Michigan scored two touchdowns and pushed the Buckeyes around for most of the first half. But then, as if drawing energy from those headbands, Ohio State rallied. The Wolverines fumbled and Ohio State manufactured a 61-yard touchdown drive off

Players wear headbands that read EARLE in support of their coach Earle Bruce in Ann Arbor, MI in 1987

the turnover. The Buckeyes were still behind 13-7, but the comeback had started.

In the second half, Buckeye quarterback Tom Tupa passed the ball to tailback Carlos Snow, who turned up field and raced down the sideline. No Michigan defender could catch him as he ran right through the end zone into the arms of a cheering Brutus Buckeye for a touchdown. Now at 14-13, the Bucks had their first lead of the game!

A touchdown and missed extra point put the Bucks ahead 20-13, but Michigan would answer back with a touchdown of their own to tie the game at 20-20. The Buckeyes would need to score again if they were going to win coach Bruce's final game.

That opportunity presented itself at the end of the fourth quarter. Ohio State moved the ball the length of the field to set up a 26-yard field goal. It was just what the Bucks needed. The ball sailed through the posts, putting Ohio State up 23-20. Now it was up to the defense to hold off a final drive from the maize and blue.

With little time left, Michigan had the ball close to midfield. A botched handoff caused their running back to fumble—and Ohio State came up holding the football! The Buckeyes ran out the clock for an emotional and memorable victory.

In his final game, Earle Bruce went out on top. The players he loved hoisted him onto their shoulders and carried him off the field, victorious in Michigan Stadium. Bruce pumped his fist, slapped some high fives and waved to the crowd. "There is no sweeter victory in the world than one over Michigan in your last game at Ohio State," he said afterward. "But the real thrill of that football game was for our football team, down 13-0, to come back and win after the week they've had." Even Michigan head coach Bo Schembechler told reporters, "I always mind losing to Ohio State, but I didn't mind so much today."

In later years, Bruce would return to Ohio State often as a mentor and grandfather figure to the football program. During a game in 2016 he dotted the *i* in the Ohio State University Marching Band's "Script Ohio" formation. Bruce pumped his fists and tipped his fedora to the cheering crowd just as he had done on top of his players' shoulders almost 30 years earlier. Time and change had surely shown that the Ohio State football team he loved so much still loved him right back.

Time Out for Tradition

Script Ohio

Script Ohio is The Ohio State University Marching Band's most well-known formation. The band marches in a single-file line, spelling "Ohio" in cursive as if a pen were writing the word. Dotting the *i* in Script Ohio is an honor usually given to a fourth- or fifth-year sousaphone player in the marching band. The band can, however, give this honor to a non-band member (it is a very special and rare event).

About The Author

Emily Stover lives in Cincinnati, Ohio. She is a graduate of The Ohio State University where she earned a Bachelor of Science in Human Ecology and a Master of Education in Elementary Education. After five years as an elementary teacher in North Olmsted City Schools, she and her husband welcomed twin girls, and she decided to stay home to raise them. Now a mother of four children (3 girls and a boy) her days are filled managing sports schedules, music lessons, clubs, and activities.

She fell in love with Ohio State Football her freshman year of college when she attended her first game seated in the very top row of C deck. Her junior year she traveled to Tempe, Arizona for the Fiesta Bowl and watched the Buckeyes win the national championship. She remembers watching "Holy Buckeye!" on TV from her off-campus college apartment. These days, she watches the games from home alongside her husband Geoff, children Ava, Kara, Ellie and Caleb, and mini goldendoodle Sadie.

"There are so many moments in Ohio State Football worthy of being told. It was my hope from the beginning of this project to share some of them with my own children in a way that brought them to life and captured their magic."

-Emily Stover

Carmen Ohio

Words By: Fred. A. Cornell, 1906
Arrangement By: Geoff Stover

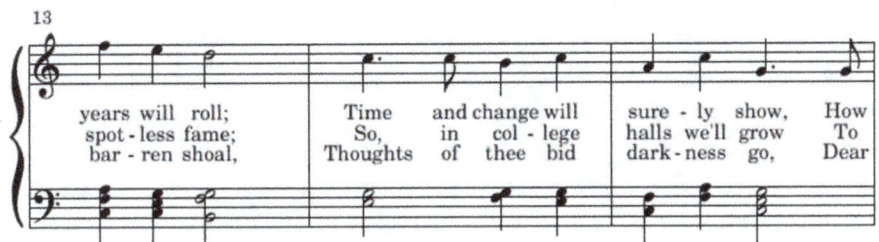

years will roll;	Time	and change will	sure - ly show,	How
spot - less fame;	So,	in col - lege	halls we'll grow	To
bar - ren shoal,	Thoughts	of thee bid	dark - ness go,	Dear

firm	thy	friend - ship	O	-	HI	-	O!
love	thee	bet - ter	O	-	HI	-	O!
Al -	ma	Ma - ter	O	-	HI	-	O!

© Photo credit: Ken Wolter / Shutterstock.com